The Ultimate Guide to Chess

Contents:

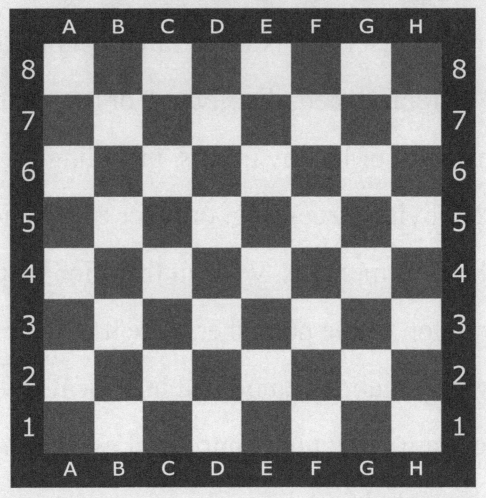

Chess is a two-player strategy game that is played on a square board with 64 squares of alternating colors. Each player starts with 16 pieces: one king, one queen, two rooks, two knights, two bishops, and eight pawns. The goal of the game is to checkmate your opponent's king, which means the king is in a position to be captured (in check) and there is no way to move the king out of capture (mate).

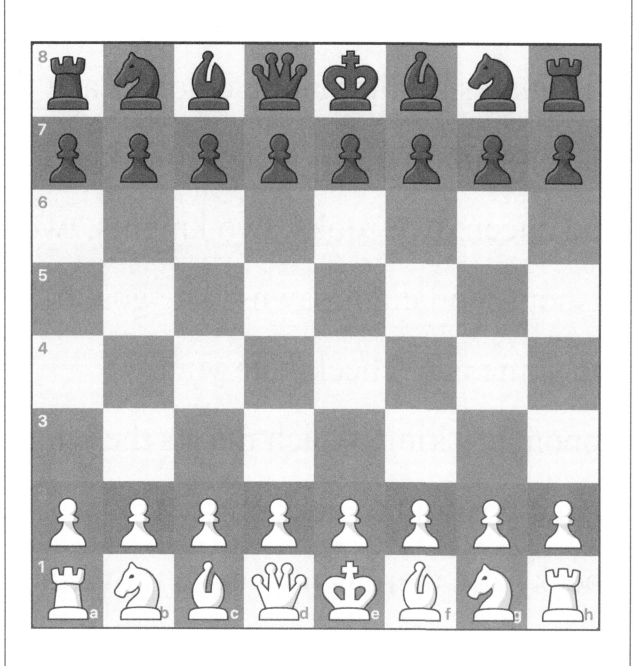

Frequently Asked Questions:

1.What are the different pieces in a game of chess? The different pieces in a game of chess are the king, queen, rooks, knights, bishops, and pawns.

2.How do you win a game of chess? You win a game of chess by placing your opponent's king in a position of capture (check) and there is no way for the opponent to move the king out of capture (mate).

3.What is castling in chess? Castling is a special move that involves the king and either rook of the same color. The king is moved two squares towards a rook on the player's first rank, then that rook moves to the square the king crossed.

Attacking Principles:

1.Control the center: The player who controls the center of the board has more space to move their pieces and greater mobility.

2.Develop your pieces: Bring all of your pieces into the game as quickly as possible to increase your attacking potential.

3.Apply pressure: Keep the pressure on your opponent's pieces and try to limit their mobility.

4.Look for weaknesses: Identify any weaknesses in your opponent's position and try to exploit them.

5.Create threats: Make threats that force your opponent to react, giving you more control over the position.

Memorization Techniques:

1.Study famous games: Study the games of grandmasters to see how they handle different positions and strategies.

2.Use flashcards: Create flashcards with different chess positions and try to recall the best move for each.

3.Practice visualization: Practice visualizing different chess positions and imagining the moves you would make.

4.Play regularly: The more you play, the more patterns and strategies you will memorize.

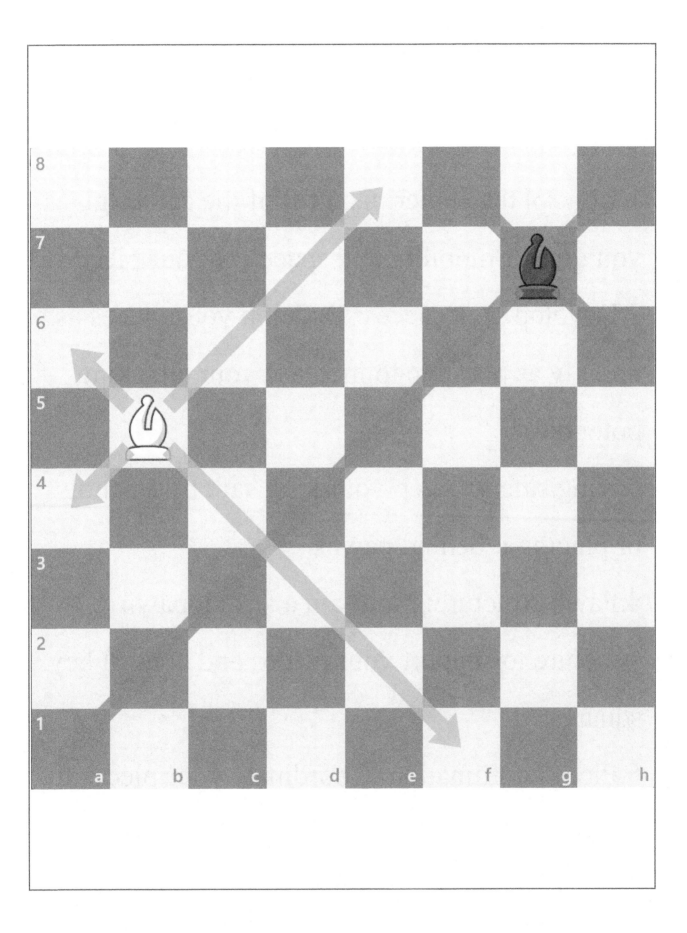

Chess Fundamentals:

1.Control the center: Control of the center gives you greater mobility and space for your pieces.

2.Develop your pieces: Develop your pieces as quickly as possible to increase your attacking potential.

3.King safety: Keep your king safe by castling or placing it behind pawns.

4.Pawn structure: Maintain a strong pawn structure to support your pieces and control key squares.

5.Piece coordination: Coordinate your pieces to work together effectively.

Chess Glossary:

1. Check: When a player's king is under attack and in danger of being captured.

2. Mate: When a king is in check and there is no way to move it out of capture.

3. Castling: A special move involving the king and rook.

4. En passant: A special pawn capture that can only be made on a player's next move after the opponent has moved a pawn two squares forward from its starting position.

5. Pin: When a piece is prevented from moving because it would expose a more valuable piece behind it to capture.

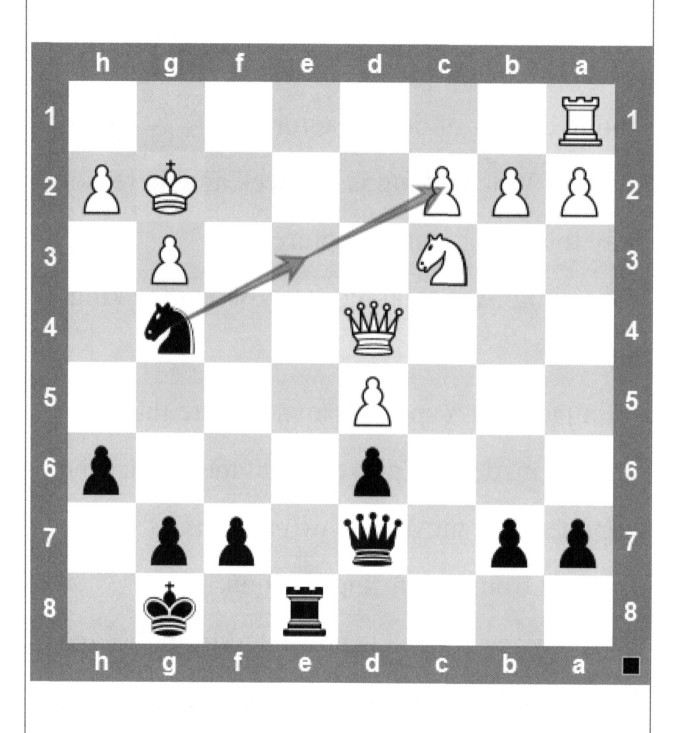

Chess Rules:

1.The game is played on a square board with 64 squares of alternating colors.

2.Each player starts with 16 pieces: one king, one queen, two rooks, two knights, two bishops, and eight pawns.

3.The goal of the game is to checkmate your opponent's king.

4.The player with the white pieces moves first, and then players alternate moves.

5.A piece can only move to an unoccupied square, or it can capture an opponent's piece by moving to a square occupied by that piece.

6.The king can only move one square in any direction, but it cannot move to a square that is attacked by an opponent's piece.

7.The queen can move in any direction, horizontally, vertically, or diagonally, as far as she likes.

8.The rook can move horizontally or vertically, as far as she likes.

9.The bishop can move diagonally, as far as he likes.

10.The knight moves in an L-shape: two squares in one direction, and then one square in a perpendicular direction. Knights are the only pieces that can "jump" over other pieces.

11.Pawns move forward one square, but capture diagonally. If a pawn reaches the opponent's end of the board, it can be promoted to a queen, rook, bishop, or knight of the same color.

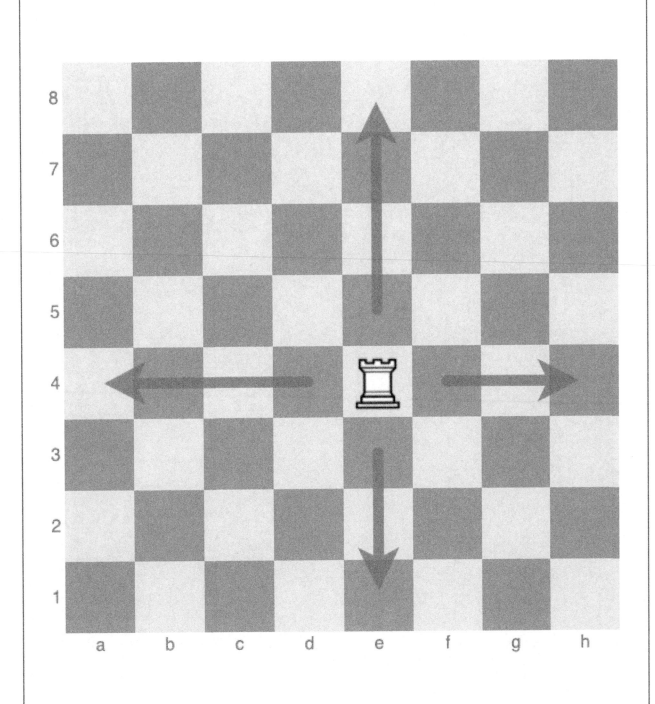

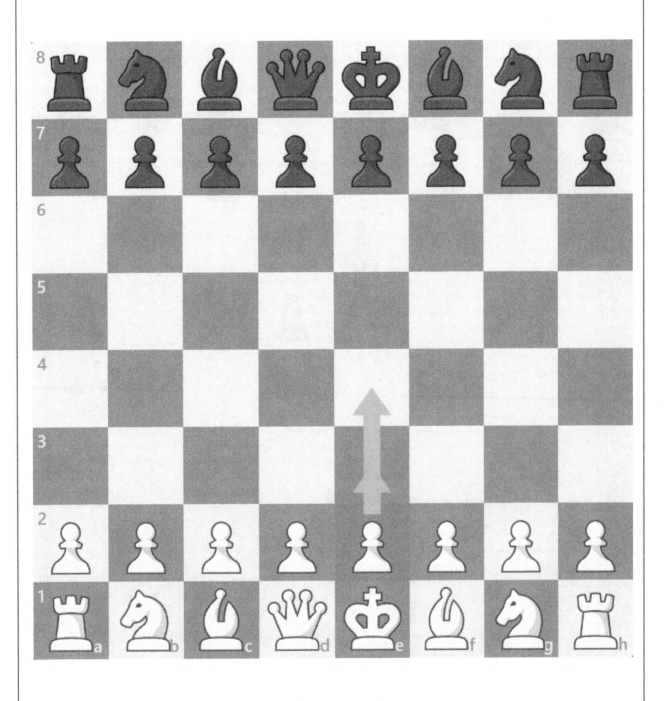

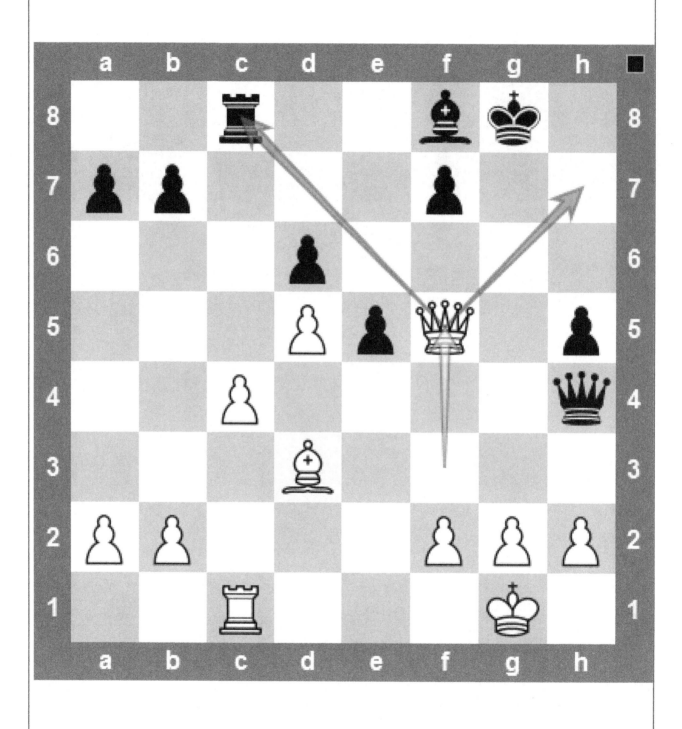

Bishops:

1.Bishops are powerful pieces that can control long diagonals on the board.

2.Bishops are most effective when they are placed on squares of their own color.

3.Bishops can work together to control the center and restrict the opponent's pieces.

4.Bishops can be used to attack the opponent's king or to defend your own king.

5.Bishops are valuable pieces, and it is usually a good idea to try to preserve them for the endgame.

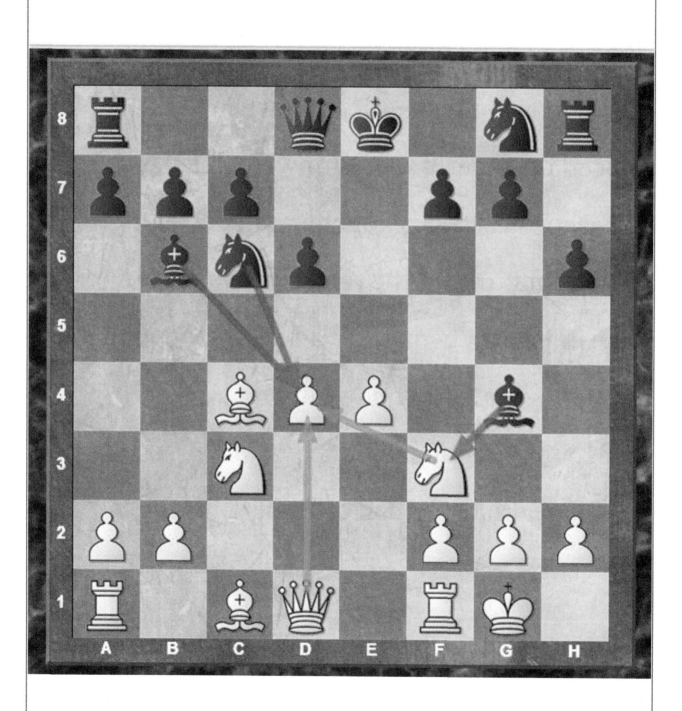

In conclusion, chess is a complex game that requires strategic thinking and planning. Understanding the different pieces, their moves, and their strengths and weaknesses is crucial to becoming a strong chess player. Also, memorizing common patterns, studying famous games, and practicing regularly are all essential to improving your chess skills. Finally, it's important to understand the importance of controlling the center, developing your pieces, keeping your king safe, maintaining a strong pawn structure, and coordinating your pieces. With practice and patience, anyone can become a skilled chess player.

Additional Resources for Further Study and Practice:

1.Books:

*"My 60 Memorable Games" by Bobby Fischer

*"The Art of Attack in Chess" by Vladimir Vukovic

*"Chess: 5334 Problems, Combinations, and Games" by Laszlo Polgar

*"The Ideas Behind the Chess Openings" by Reuben Fine

2.Online resources:

*Chess.com: an online platform for playing chess, watching tutorials, and participating in tournaments

*Lichess.org: a free, ad-free, and open-source online chess platform

*YouTube: a wealth of instructional videos and tutorials from top chess players and coaches

*Chessgames.com: a database of historic chess games and matches, along with annotations and analysis

3.Practice with a chess computer:

*Use chess software or play against a chess computer to practice your skills and learn new strategies.

4.Participate in chess tournaments:

*Join local chess clubs and participate in tournaments to test your skills against other players.

5.Study with a coach or mentor:

*Consider working with a chess coach or mentor to receive personalized instruction and guidance.

Printed in Great Britain
by Amazon

35230652R00020